Francis Frith's
Sussex

Photographic Memories

Francis Frith's
Sussex

Martin Andrew

First published in the United Kingdom in 1998
by WBC Ltd

Revised paperback edition published in the United Kingdom in 2000 by
The Francis Frith Collection
ISBN 1-85937-184-1

Reprinted in paperback 2001, 2003, 2006

British Library Cataloguing in Publication Data

Sussex Photographic Memories
Martin Andrew

The Francis Frith Collection
Frith's Barn, Teffont,
Salisbury, Wiltshire SP3 5QP
Tel: +44 (0) 1722 716 376
Email: info@francisfrith.co.uk
www.francisfrith.com

Printed and bound in Great Britain

Front Cover: **Brighton**, *The Beach 1898* 41890t

*The colour-tinting is for illustrative purposes only, and
is not intended to be historically accurate*

AS WITH ANY HISTORICAL DATABASE THE FRITH ARCHIVE IS CONSTANTLY BEING CORRECTED AND IMPROVED
AND THE PUBLISHERS WOULD WELCOME INFORMATION ON OMISSIONS OR INACCURACIES

Contents

Francis Frith: *Victorian Pioneer*

FRANCIS FRITH, Victorian founder of the world-famous photographic archive, was a complex and multitudinous man. A devout Quaker and a highly successful Victorian businessman, he was both philosophic by nature and pioneering in outlook.

By 1855 Francis Frith had already established a wholesale grocery business in Liverpool, and sold it for the astonishing sum of £200,000, which is the equivalent today of over £15,000,000. Now a very rich man, he was able to indulge his passion for travel. As a child he had pored over travel books written by early explorers, and his fancy and imagination had been stirred by family holidays to the sublime mountain regions of Wales and Scotland. 'What lands of spirit-stirring and enriching scenes and places!' he had written. He was to return to these scenes of grandeur in later years to 'recapture the thousands of vivid and tender memories', but with a different purpose. Now in his thirties, and captivated by the new science of photography, Frith set out on a series of pioneering journeys to the Nile regions that occupied him from 1856 until 1860.

Intrigue and Adventure

He took with him on his travels a specially-designed wicker carriage that acted as both dark-room and sleeping chamber. These far-flung journeys were packed with intrigue and adventure. In his life story, written when he was sixty-three, Frith tells of being held captive by bandits, and of fighting 'an awful midnight battle to the very point of surrender with a deadly pack of hungry, wild dogs'. Sporting flowing Arab costume, Frith arrived at Akaba by camel sixty years before Lawrence, where he encountered 'desert princes and rival sheikhs, blazing with jewel-hilted swords'.

During these extraordinary adventures he was assiduously exploring the desert regions bordering the Nile and patiently recording the antiquities and peoples with his camera. He was the first photographer to venture beyond the sixth cataract. Africa was still the mysterious 'Dark Continent', and Stanley and Livingstone's historic meeting was a decade into the future. The conditions for picture taking confound belief. He laboured for hours in his wicker dark-room in the sweltering heat of the desert, while the volatile chemicals fizzed dangerously in their trays. Often he was forced to work in remote tombs and caves where conditions were cooler. Back in London he exhibited his photographs and was 'rapturously cheered' by members of the Royal Society. His reputation as a photographer was made overnight. An eminent modern historian has likened their impact on the population of the time to that on our own generation of the first photographs taken on the surface of the moon.

Venture of a Life-Time

Characteristically, Frith quickly spotted the opportunity to create a new business as a specialist publisher of photographs. He lived in an era of immense and sometimes violent change. For the poor in the early part of Victoria's reign work was a drudge and the hours long, and people had precious little free time to enjoy themselves. Most had no transport other than a cart or gig at their disposal, and had not travelled far beyond

the boundaries of their own town or village. However, by the 1870s, the railways had threaded their way across the country, and Bank Holidays and half-day Saturdays had been made obligatory by Act of Parliament. All of a sudden the ordinary working man and his family were able to enjoy days out and see a little more of the world.

With characteristic business acumen, Francis Frith foresaw that these new tourists would enjoy having souvenirs to commemorate their days out. In 1860 he married Mary Ann Rosling and set out with the intention of photographing every city, town and village in Britain. For the next thirty years he travelled the country by train and by pony and trap, producing fine photographs of seaside resorts and beauty spots that were keenly bought by millions of Victorians. These prints were painstakingly pasted into family albums and pored over during the dark nights of winter, rekindling precious memories of summer excursions.

The Rise of Frith & Co

Frith's studio was soon supplying retail shops all over the country. To meet the demand he gathered about him a small team of photographers, and published the work of independent artist-photographers of the calibre of Roger Fenton and Francis Bedford. In order to gain some understanding of the scale of Frith's business one only has to look at the catalogue issued by Frith & Co in 1886: it runs to some 670 pages, listing not only many thousands of views of the British Isles but also many photographs of most European countries, and China, Japan, the USA and

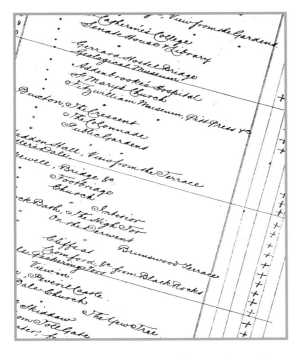

Canada – note the sample page shown above from the hand-written *Frith & Co* ledgers detailing pictures taken. By 1890 Frith had created the greatest specialist photographic publishing company in the world, with over 2,000 outlets – more than the combined number that Boots and WH Smith have today! The picture on the right shows the *Frith & Co* display board at Ingleton in the Yorkshire Dales (left of window). Beautifully constructed with a mahogany frame and gilt inserts, it could display up to a dozen local scenes.

Postcard Bonanza

The ever-popular holiday postcard we know today took many years to develop. In 1870 the Post Office issued the first plain cards, with a pre-printed stamp on one face. In 1894 they allowed other publishers' cards to be sent through the mail with an attached adhesive halfpenny stamp. Demand grew rapidly, and

in 1895 a new size of postcard was permitted called the court card, but there was little room for illustration. In 1899, a year after Frith's death, a new card measuring 5.5 x 3.5 inches became the standard format, but it was not until 1902 that the divided back came into being, with address and message on one face and a full-size illustration on the other. *Frith & Co* were in the vanguard of postcard development, and Frith's sons Eustace and Cyril continued their father's monumental task, expanding the number of views offered to the public and recording more and more places in Britain, as the coasts and countryside were opened up to mass travel.

Francis Frith died in 1898 at his villa in Cannes, his great project still growing. The archive he created continued in business for another seventy years. By 1970 it contained over a third of a million pictures of 7,000 cities, towns and villages. The massive photographic record Frith has left to us stands as a living monument to a special and very remarkable man.

Frith's Archive: *A Unique Legacy*

FRANCIS FRITH'S legacy to us today is of immense significance and value, for the magnificent archive of evocative photographs he created provides a unique record of change in 7,000 cities, towns and villages throughout Britain over a century and more. Frith and his fellow studio photographers revisited locations many times down the years to update their views, compiling for us an enthralling and colourful pageant of British life and character.

We tend to think of Frith's sepia views of Britain as nostalgic, for most of us use them to conjure up memories of places in our own lives with which we have family associations. It often makes us forget that to Francis Frith they were records of daily life as it was actually being lived in the cities, towns and villages of his day. The Victorian age was one of great and often bewildering change for ordinary people,

and though the pictures evoke an impression of slower times, life was as busy and hectic as it is today.

We are fortunate that Frith was a photographer of the people, dedicated to recording the minutiae of everyday life. For it is this sheer wealth of visual data, the painstaking chronicle of changes in dress, transport, street layouts, buildings, housing, engineering and landscape that captivates us so much today. His remarkable images offer us a powerful link with the past and with the lives of our ancestors.

Today's Technology

Computers have now made it possible for Frith's many thousands of images to be accessed almost instantly. In the Frith archive today, each photograph is carefully 'digitised' then stored on a CD Rom. Frith archivists can locate a single photograph amongst thousands within seconds. Views can be catalogued and sorted under a variety of categories of place and content to the immediate benefit of researchers.

Inexpensive reference prints can be created for them at the touch of a mouse button, and a wide range of books and other printed materials assembled and published for a wider, more general readership. The day-to-day workings of the archive are very different from how they were in Francis Frith's time: imagine the herculean task of sorting through eleven tons of glass negatives as Frith had to do to locate a particular sequence of pictures! Yet the archive still prides itself on maintaining the same high

See Frith at www.francisfrith.com

standards of excellence laid down by Francis Frith, including the painstaking cataloguing and indexing of every view.

It is curious to reflect on how the internet now allows researchers in America and elsewhere greater instant access to the archive than Frith himself ever enjoyed. Many thousands of individual views can be called up on screen within seconds on one of the Frith internet sites, enabling people living continents away to revisit the streets of their ancestral home town, or view places in Britain where they have enjoyed holidays. Many overseas researchers welcome the chance to view special theme selections, such as transport, sports, costume and ancient monuments.

We are certain that Francis Frith would have heartily approved of these modern developments in imaging techniques, for he himself was always working at the very limits of Victorian photographic technology.

The Value of the Archive Today

Because of the benefits brought by the computer, Frith's images are increasingly studied by social historians, by researchers into genealogy and ancestory, by architects, town planners, and by teachers and schoolchildren involved in local history projects.

In addition, the archive offers every one of us an opportunity to examine the places where we and our families have lived and worked down the years. Highly successful in Frith's own era, the archive is now, a century and more on, entering a new phase of popularity.

The Past in Tune with the Future

Historians consider the Francis Frith Collection to be of prime national importance. It is the only archive of its kind remaining in private ownership and has been valued at a million pounds. However, this figure is now rapidly increasing as digital technology enables more and more people around the world to enjoy its benefits.

Francis Frith's archive is now housed in an historic timber barn in the beautiful village of Teffont in Wiltshire. Its founder would not recognize the archive office as it is today. In place of the many thousands of dusty boxes containing glass plate negatives and an all-pervading odour of photographic chemicals, there are now ranks of computer screens. He would be amazed to watch his images travelling round the world at unimaginable speeds through network and internet lines.

The archive's future is both bright and exciting. Francis Frith, with his unshakeable belief in making photographs available to the greatest number of people, would undoubtedly approve of what is being done today with his lifetime's work. His photographs, depicting our shared past, are now bringing pleasure and enlightenment to millions around the world a century and more after his death.

Ancient Ports and the Working Sea

Bosham 1903 50912
Bosham features on the Bayeux Tapestry, for in 1064 Harold sailed from Bosham to Normandy, and set in train the events that led to the Battle of Hastings and his own death. Much of the church that he built still survives, surrounded by this prosperous village and its yachting harbour. A century ago Bosham was still a working fishing port. This view is taken from what is now the Bosham Yacht Club quay looking east at high tide.

Hastings, The Net Drying Sheds c1955 H36018
These tall weatherboarded net 'shops' (net drying sheds) cluster on the foreshore below East Cliff. They are of varying dates, and there are a remarkable number of them - a fascinating reminder, of Hastings' importance as a fishing port.

Hastings, The Castle 1925 77968

In 1066, William, Duke of Normandy, having landed at Pevensey to claim the English throne from King Harold, marched here and built a timber castle. One of the medieval Cinque Ports, Hastings remained a fishing port until relatively recently. These ruins are all that remain of the Norman castle and former church of St Mary on West Cliff, most of which disappeared into the sea when the cliffs were washed away during ferocious storms in 1287.

Newhaven, High Street 1890 27760

The town was never remarkable architecturally, although there were some attractive 18th- and 19th-century buildings in the High Street. Many survive, greatly altered, and the street is now partly pedestrianised.

◀ **Newhaven
The Church 1890**
27763
The church has a central Norman tower with an apsidal chancel to its east. The spire is splay-footed, the pyramidal cap being chamfered away from the base to form eight sides.

◄ **Newhaven**
The Harbour c1960 N20054
Despite its name, Newhaven is anything but new, for it dates from Henry VIII's time when the River Ouse was canalised into its present course, and the town absorbed the old village of Meeching. After 1850, the arrival of the railway revived the port to its present bustle. Later 19th-century harbour works were an attempt to rival Dover in the cross Channel trade: the Newhaven-Dieppe ferry still steams from here.

▼ **Newhaven**
Lewes Road 1890
27762
The Lewes Road used to be the main route out of town, but this is now along the east bank of the Ouse towards Lewes. This peaceful scene is now barely recognisable.

◄ **Rye**
Looking over Romney Marshes c1955 R77102
This unspoilt walled town on its hilltop site was an important port until Elizabethan times, when the sea abandoned it and its harbour silted up. Looking across the Ypres Tower from the parish church roof, the marshes are much bleaker than now, with the Rother winding through the treeless flat land. Where the cars are parked houses have reappeared.

Rye
The River Rother
1901 47445
In the 1190s Rye joined
the Cinque Ports
federation, a group of
Kent and Sussex ports
that provided ships for
the King's navy in return
for enormous privileges.
The two-masted fishing
boats in the foreground,
as we look west from
the River Rother, are
reminders that Rye was
a working port, not
merely the genteel town
the tourists now see.

Rye, Ypres Castle 1912 64929
The Ypres Tower of c1250 was sold in 1430 to John de Ypres as a house. This is inexplicable, bearing in mind the French raid of 1377. A prison from 1518 to 1865, it is now a museum.

Rye, The Landgate 1890 25405
This is the only one of the four town gates that survived. Dating from 1329 or 1381, it had a portcullis and a drawbridge, and is a most imposing entrance to the town.

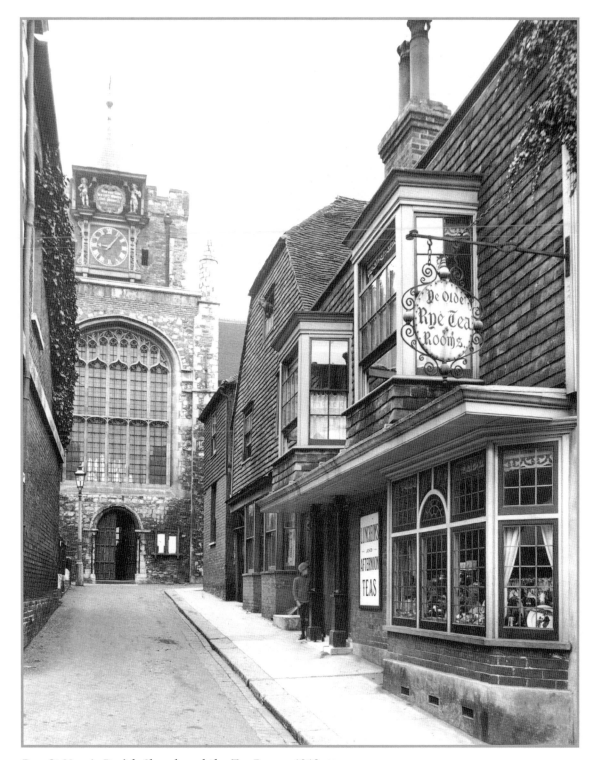

Rye, St Mary's Parish Church and the Tea Rooms 1912 64923
The quarter boys above the church clock date from 1761, while the tea rooms (now Simon the Pieman, established in 1920 after this view was taken) replaced the Red Lion Inn which burned down in 1872.

▼ Rye, The Town Hall 1901 47459

The Town Hall was designed by Andrews Jelfe, a London master mason in 1743. On Mayoring Day the council members and guests, somewhat unkindly, throw heated pennies to the crowd from the upper windows.

▼ Rye, Mermaid Street 1888 21161

This is the most famous street in Rye. The immaculate gabled timber-framed house, built as Hartshorne House in 1576, was described in 1863 as 'too dilapidated to allow the lowest to find shelter beneath its roof'.

▲ Rye
West Street 1888 21159

Thomas House, the timber-framed building on the left, has been well restored, while the corner house was replaced in 1920 by a brick and tile-hung Neo-Georgian Lloyds Bank, a most attractive building fronting the High Street.

◄ **Rye**
Camber Castle 1894
34446
Isolated in the flat fields
south of Rye, Camber
Castle, one of Henry VIII's
coastal forts of the 1540s,
is now over a mile from the
retreating sea: well beyond
Tudor artillery range.

Selsey, The Life Boat House 1930 83449
Unlike Rye, the medieval town of Selsey lies below sea level owing to coastal erosion. It was the seat of an Anglo-Saxon bishopric, hence the local legend of a cathedral under the sea. A life boat was established here in 1861, and this one was replaced in 1960 by a larger version of the same design. Lobster pots, small fishing boats and flint cobble walled fishermen's cottages survive the tide of modern housing.

Winchelsea 1906 53491
Old Winchelsea was washed away in late 13th-century storms, and in 1287 the citizens moved to the new town laid out on a hill. However, the harbour silted up and the town declined rapidly, and its present atmosphere is more that of a very attractive village. The 1831 Wellhouse on the left incorporates medieval archways; the pyramid-roofed building is the wellhouse itself. At the far right is the chancel of St Thomas's Church.

Winchelsea, Castle Street 1912 64944
This view gives an idea of the regular and spacious layout of the town. Most houses are 17th- and 18th-century, but over thirty medieval undercrofts or cellars survive; they were used for storing Bordeaux wines, the basis of its trade.

The Sussex Seaside 1850-1914

Bexhill, The Parade 1903 50308
The Dutch gables on the hotels and apartments are typical of Bexhill's Victorian architecture, although the seaside buildings favour the Moorish look: provincial and dim echoes of the Brighton Pavilion perhaps?

Bexhill
The Sea Front 1903
50306

The Moorish minareted building has gone, as have the elegant gates, the brick and stone archway, and the gate piers. Bexhill now has the 1930s De La Warr Pavilion, an elegant concrete and glass building of great beauty.

Bexhill
The Old Town 1897 38994

While the old town up the hill had its origins in the 8th century, the Bexhill everyone knows grew up from the 1880s by the sea as a resort on Earl De La Warr's estate. Thus its architectural character is more late Victorian than the Regency stucco of Brighton. The tree has gone and motor cars have arrived, but the buildings of the old town on its hill survive almost intact, a charming mix of brick, painted weatherboarding and flint.

Bognor Regis
The Parade and the Pier 1911 63793

Stagnation ended when the railway arrived, and in 1910 Bognor got a new pier, which had just been completed at the time this view was taken. The pier building's tall seaward end has now gone, and the pier beyond it has been closed following extensive storm damage.

Bognor Regis
The Steyne 1921 71463

Every south coast town had to have its 'Steyne', copying the name from Brighton. Bognor's is a delight, with stucco cottages of varying heights and designs, many with balconied bow and bay windows, fronting an elongated square.

**Bognor Regis
The Beach 1890** 22626
Bognor's growth from a tiny fishing village started in the 1780s, with Sir Richard Hotham's grand scheme inland (immodestly named Hothampton) aimed at the nobility and gentry, but was followed by piecemeal Regency and later growth along the sea front. The casual way Bognor developed is brought out well in this view, with no two buildings the same or related to each other. Horse-drawn bathing machines were still in use to safeguard bathers' modesty.

Bognor Regis, High Street 1890 22633
Apart from the old post office, much of the left-hand side survives, but on the right only The William Hardwicke pub remains amid rebuilding, including the 1930s Bobby's department store, after which the 1960s did their worst.

Brighton, The Pavilion 1889 22244
Once a fishing village, Brighton was rescued by the late 18th-century fashion for sea air and sea bathing. Only five hours from London, and endorsed by the Prince Regent, the town spread along the coast in stucco waves. This astonishing building started life as a farmhouse, then became a classical villa with a rotunda, before Nash transformed it into this domed and minareted Mahatman-Indian palace for the Prince Regent.

Brighton, The Beach 1898 41890
This view brings out the tremendous bustle of Brighton's beaches, dotted with small sailing boats and lines of bathing machines. In the background is the Palace Pier, the chain pier's replacement, under construction: this photograph freezes a moment in history.

Brighton, The Aquarium 1889 22238
Richard Jefferies described Brighton's special quality of sun, wind and light in the 1880s: 'The wind coming up the cliff seems to bring with it whole armfuls of sunshine, and to throw the warmth and light against you as you linger ... light and wind spring upwards from the pavement ... the sky is richly blue against the parapets overhead.'

◄ **Brighton
The Chain Pier, 1870**
B208003
After the railway arrived, Brighton's continued popularity was assured. Designed by Captain Samuel Brown in 1823, the pier was like a four-span suspension bridge, jutting about 1,000 ft into the sea. Featuring in a painting by Turner, it was swept away in storms in 1896.

◄ **Brighton
The Beach 1902** 48516
From Palace Pier looking east, beyond the terminus of Magnus Volks' 1883 Electric Railway, we can see the late 1890s arches of Madeira Terrace, halfway up the sea wall in front of Marine Parade, with Kemp Town in the distance.

▼ **Brighton
The Beach and Boat, 1889** 22345
Besides watching clowns, jugglers, musicians and conjurors, short sea trips in the little sailing boats were immensely popular. West Pier in the background looks just like it did when it first opened in 1866 before later additions and alterations.

◄ **Brighton
The 'Skylark' Sets Sail 1902** 48504
In 1902 it's 'All aboard the Skylark', as a party set out in the little gaff-rigged yawl with its crew of two. In the background, West Pier has now received its continuous and necessary central wind screen.

**Brighton
The West Pier 1902**
48495
West Pier, now sadly derelict and awaiting restoration, was enlarged at the seaward end in 1890 to accommodate a larger pavilion. The ships tied up at the seaward end show the original function of seaside piers.

▼ **Brighton, The Old Steyne 1902** 48522
Once marshy common used for drying fishing nets, The Steyne was
drained and turned into elegant gardens. Surrounded by fashionable
tall lodging houses, it provided a more sheltered alternative
promenade to the windy sea front.

▼ **Brighton, The Metropole Hotel 1890** 27610
Rearing out amid the stucco, the bright red brick and terra-cotta of
Alfred Waterhouse's 1890 Metropole Hotel must have seemed
remarkably intrusive when it was first built. The 1860s Grand Hotel on
the right is in Italianate stucco.

▲ **Brighton
The Palace Pier 1902**
48513
Widely considered the
finest pier ever built, it
was designed by R St
Moore, and opened in
1899; the theatre at the
end was added in 1901.
As usual, an exotic hybrid
of Turkish-Oriental-Arabic
style was selected.

◄ **Brighton
Laying Tram Lines
in North Road c1904**
B208002
After the Volks Electric
Railway on the sea front
was licensed in 1883, the
Corporation eventually
followed around 1900 with
its own electric tram
system. Here, tram lines are
being laid along North
Road from Grand Parade.

The Devil's Dyke 1902 48527
When tiring of the cosmopolitan delights of the town, visitors could climb onto the South Downs and enjoy sublime views. The Devil's Dyke was a popular destination, allegedly dug by the Devil to flood the Weald.

Eastbourne, The Parade 1899 43938
By the 1880s, Eastbourne became 'The Empress of Watering Places', set against the backdrop of Beachy Head. In the distance is the Wish Tower, one of the Martello tower fortlets built during the Napoleonic Wars. Apart from the small villa, the Italianate stucco terrace houses of the 1850s and later mostly remain.

Eastbourne, The Old Town 1890 25329
Eastbourne owes its development to the seventh Duke of Devonshire: after the railway arrived in 1849, he enthusiastically developed his estates here into a huge resort, with nearly three miles of seafront. The old town was engulfed; of the buildings in this view, only the old parish church, seen in the distance, survives. Out of view, much of the old town still stands, including the Lamb, a fine medieval timber-framed building.

Eastbourne, On The Sands 1910 62959
Behind the somewhat overdressed children is Eastbourne's fine pier, designed by Eugenius Birch in 1871. The end building with its dome and pinnacles dates from 1888.

**Eastbourne
The Pier 1912** 64968
The domed concert hall at the far end seems like an oriental palace, an effect heightened by the octagonal domed entrance kiosks, straight from the Top-Kapi Palace in Istanbul - a joyous contrast to all that Italianate stucco.

▼ **Eastbourne, The Town Hall 1894** 34472
Eastbourne, to befit its new status, built itself a splendidly showy
and grand town hall in the 1880s. The town fathers imported a
Birmingham architect, W Tadman Foulkes, who did them proud: what
a wonderful tower.

▼ **Hastings, The Esplanade 1890** 25353
Hastings emerged as a seaside resort in the early 19th century, and expanded
rapidly from its kernel of a fishing port and town. In this view from the pier
virtually all the houses still survive, many now in a state of serious decay
and others drastically altered. In the early morning the jaunty striped bathing
machines await business.

▲ **Hastings
From East Cliff 1891**
29039
The picturesque cliffs,
coves, glens and wooded
scenery that surround
Hastings appealed to the
Romantic tastes of the
years after 1800. This
panoramic view shows
how the town is hemmed
in by sandstone cliffs.
Below, in the foreground,
are the fishing boats, net
drying sheds and nets
drying in the open air;
the net shops are unique
reminders of the
fishermen of the town.
The resort starts beyond
them.

◄ **Hastings**
The Pier 1890 22780
The Turkish palace-style pier of 1872 has onion-domed kiosks and an elegant promenade above the water to a romantic Sultan's palace. The pier has since been much built on, with varying degrees of success.

Hastings, The Lifeboat House 1894 34427
The elegant Victorian life boat house with its round tower and conical roof, quite new at this time, has now gone, and a modern concrete life boat station replaces it further south-east, painted an attractive blue.

Hastings, Fairlight Glen 1890 22804
Fairlight Glen, two miles east of the town, was a particularly popular walk destination with its romantic sandstone scenery and deep cut valleys or 'glens', a suitably Walter Scottish image. It is now a country park.

Hastings, Ecclesbourne Glen 1890 25377
Part of Hastings' early success was due to the picturesque scenery beyond the town to the east, with rugged coastal scenery deep cut with glens, woodland walks and cliff paths.

◄ **Hove**
The Drive 1898 41895
Hove, a small fishing village west of Brighton, developed slowly from the mid 19th century onwards. As at Brighton, large areas of working class housing arose away from the sea front. The Drive is typical of the development of the Stanford Estate after 1871: yellow brick semi-detached villas with cement dressings, slate roofs and bay windows in wide tree-lined streets - totally different from Hove's earlier grand stucco terraces.

◀ **Hove**
Church Road and the Town Hall 1898 41896
Always jealous of its independence, Hove evaded big brother Brighton's dominance and obtained borough status in 1898. Waterhouse, the architect of The Metropole Hotel, designed a splendid red brick and terracotta Town Hall in 1882. Tragically, it burnt down in 1966, and a modern structure took its place. The gasholder and the commercial buildings still remain.

▼ **Littlehampton**
High Street 1892 29970
A port at the mouth of the Arun, and once a Tudor royal shipyard, the old town runs east from the river bank. Further east is the seaside resort, built soon after 1800 in stucco terraces with Waterloo balconies. Not until late Victorian times did the two parts merge. This view is virtually unchanged, apart from the loss of the trees and renewed shop fronts. People can still wander down the middle of the road, for it is now pedestrianised.

◀ **Littlehampton**
South Terrace 1890
22665
Although called a terrace, the houses are by numerous builders and unified by broad style alone. The grand corner house has lost its Waterloo balcony and garden railings now, but most of the others are intact.

**Littlehampton
The Promenade 1903**
50215
The early 19th-century stucco houses in the distance show how far back from the shore line the early development was. Perhaps the bleakness of the picture explains the current trees and planting, which shield the houses from sea breezes.

▼ St Leonards, From the Boundary 1891 29605

Started as New Hastings by James Burton and his architect son Decimus in 1828, and later renamed St Leonards, this seaside resort is a grand composition of palatial stucco terraces. Monumental Tuscan boundary arches were built as entrances to the estate. The pier has long gone; also destroyed is the wonderful entrance archway, its location marked by a stone with a plaque.

▼ Worthing, The Esplanade 1890 22706

In 1798 Princess Amelia gave Worthing a genteel cachet, but coastal erosion (only cured by groynes) and early sewage problems probably prevented the town rivalling Brighton in popularity. This dignified four-storey stucco terrace of about 1870, with its continuous first-floor balcony, was at the south-east corner of The Steyne. Its site is now a car park, which, let us hope, will be developed soon.

▲ Worthing
The Beach 1890 22678

Worthing, yet another fishing village turned seaside resort, developed in fits and starts with little overall coherence but some attractive accents. As we look west from the pier, we can see how patchy and sporadic the growth of Worthing was. Early 19th-century bow-fronted and balconied houses jostle with mid-Victorian Italianate stucco at varying heights and scales.

◀ **Worthing**
The Beach 1903 50079
This view looks eastwards
from the pier. The gap in
the buildings marks the
south side of the green,
down the middle of The
Steyne, laid out in 1807; it
copied that in Brighton and
borrowed its name.

Worthing, The Parade 1903 50080
The elegant late-Victorian bandstand has now been replaced by The Lido, which offers the audience protection from the elements and traffic noise. Modern buildings also replace most of those on the left of the view.

Worthing, South Street 1895 35075
The towered and porticoed Town Hall which closes the vista, a fine Classical building of 1834, subsequently lost its tower and has now been completely demolished: this is a great loss to the town's architecture and to its townscape.

Worthing, Children on the Sands 1906 56709
The older girls do not seem to have what might be termed 'holiday clothes', and one boy appears to be in school uniform complete with cap - but they are obviously enjoying themselves.

The Sussex Seaside 1914-1960

Bognor Regis, The Sea Front 1921 71438
The story goes that 'Bugger Bognor' were King
George V's last words when threatened with
another recuperation near this seaside resort.
Unfortunately, the town had much of its heart
punched out by 1960s development. The 1897
Diamond Jubilee drinking fountain was reerected in
The Steyne gardens in 1969. The pier buildings are
a shadow of their 1920s glory, with turrets gone,
windows blocked and the tallest part demolished.

◄ **Angmering Willohayne Avenue c1955** A327011
Typical of the suburban development along the coast between Littlehampton and Worthing, Willowhayne Avenue, although labelled Angmering-on-Sea, is actually in East Preston: presumably a name with more cachet. Of old East Preston, a few flinty cottages remain.

◄ **Angmering**
The Village c1955 A52009
Angmering-on-Sea is one of those suburbs that blossomed along the south coast between the wars, partly as holiday homes, and partly as homes for London commuters. As a consequence, the coast is almost completely built up between Bognor and Newhaven. The old village centre is separated from the seaside expansion. Church Street, in typical Sussex brick and flint, runs from the medieval church to The Lamb Inn.

▼ **Angmering**
Beach Chalets c1955
A327020
Doubtless state-of-the-art in 1955, these flat-roofed terraced beach huts typify the immense popularity of the post-War summer seaside holiday and day trips, but have long been demolished.

◄ **Brighton**
Sheepcote Valley Municipal Camping Ground c1955 B208510
Between the wars, Brighton boomed: by the mid-1930s it was packed at weekends. After the war, Brighton and other Sussex towns were still popular for holidays, but in the 1960s package tours took the tourists abroad. This view is a splendid evocation of 1950s holiday-making, with plywood caravans and canvas ridge tents.

Brighton, The Black Rock Bathing Pool c1955 B208508
This, the town's only open-air swimming pool, was recently demolished and replaced by the Marina and a supermarket: something of a poor exchange. In the distance along the cliffs looms Roedean, the girls' public school.

Brighton, North Street c1955 B208501
Between the wars, North and West Streets and Queen's Road developed as Brighton's shopping and commercial centre. North Street's commercial grandeur is interspersed by older buildings, including the porticoed former Clarence Hotel of 1785 and the Chapel Royal.

Camber, Holiday Chalets c1955 C436003
Sussex beaches are mostly shingle above high water mark, so it is understandable that the two miles of golden sand between the mouth of the River Rother and the shingle banks of Dungeness should develop as a holiday resort. At various points from Selsey, to Middleton to Camber, collections of ephemeral-looking buildings sprang up, some assembled from parts of railway carriages, or in fact from anything to hand.

Eastbourne, Terminus Road 1925 77963
Terminus Road, laid out in 1850, became a major commercial thoroughfare in the town, and the massive Baroque domed building on the left, sadly now demolished, symbolises the prosperity and pride of the town earlier this century.

Eastbourne
The Pier 1925 77946
Between the wars
Eastbourne continued
to expand, and until the
1950s it enjoyed great
prosperity. Its gradual
decline in the face of
the foreign package
tour has been arrested,
and it has a large
resident population. The
town has also
developed as a
conference centre. Two
immaculate charabancs,
vehicles so evocative of
pre-war leisure and
day-tripping, have just
arrived at the pier,
which now has a domed
theatre added and
reworked kiosks.

**Hastings
The Beach 1925** 77979
Hastings has suffered
very much in recent
years, now that the
boom holiday period of
the 1920s to the late
1950s has ended. Many
of the seafront houses
are in serious decay.
By the 1920s the
bathing machines had
gone. Carlisle Parade,
the enormously long
stucco terrace, is now
truncated, and the mid-
dle section has been
replaced by flat-roofed
brown brick flats of total
incongruity.

▼ Hastings, The Beach, Looking towards East Cliff c1960 H36021

Although efforts are now being made to revive the tourist trade, Hastings has a long way to go to recapture its former glory. Perched at the cliff top, the castle-like structure belongs to the East Cliff Railway. Its bright red and yellow cars are now hauled up its near vertical gradient by electricity, but it was built as a water-balance railway.

▼ Hove, The Parade 1921 71501

Hove's genteel grandeur continued to appeal to those who found Brighton somewhat too lively, and the town expanded north into the Downs in tides of suburban housing. Hove's more genteel atmosphere comes over in this view. Behind the spacious promenade are the superb 1820s stucco compositions of Brunswick Square and Terrace and Adelaide Terrace beyond, all rather like Nash's Regents Park in London.

**▲ Lancing
Golden Sands Beach
Bungalows c1955**

L11033

The Golden Sands were of course only exposed at low tide beyond the shingle, but as a name for the beach it was a winner, combined with plentiful parking on the greensward behind the beach huts.

◄ **Lancing**
South Street c1955 L11002
The ancient village of
Lancing, now by-passed by
the A27, is swallowed up by
suburban sprawl which is
continuous south to the sea.
It is another Sussex coastal
suburb nurtured by the
Southern Electric commuter
line to London. The Lancing
and District Estate Agency
turns the corner in splendid
colourwashed Moderne or
Art Deco style, symbolising
the new vibrant Inter-War
architecture.

St Leonards, Marine Court c1955 H36029
St Leonards has not sunk as low as parts of Hastings, but its edges are distinctly blurred with suburban and artisan housing swamping the areas to the north and west and, indeed, virtually merging with Bexhill. Love it or hate it, Marine Court of 1937 dominates St Leonards; like a beached ocean liner, it can be seen for miles. Thirteen storeys high, it must be the most incongruous and brutal insult to the long-suffering Sussex coastline.

Worthing, The Beach 1925 78826

Between the wars, Worthing lost its wonderful town hall and theatre. The shopping streets were modernised, but parts survived into modern times, when older buildings are more appreciated; however, the suburbs and absorbed villages make the effort of getting into the town centre a dispiriting one. The crowd are watching an event from the beach and the pier. The first 1862 pier had been rebuilt in 1889, and again in 1914 when disastrous storms turned the South Pavilion into an island.

Worthing, The Bandstand 1921 71445

Curiously, the deck chairs face away from the band playing in the ornate late Victorian bandstand, now replaced by the more sheltered Lido. Eight years later, the South Pavilion at the end of the pier was destroyed by fire.

◀ **Worthing
The Broadway 1919**

68989

Built in 1901, the somewhat overblown shop and apartment blocks, with its onion-domed corner turret, peer down The Steyne through the trees. Indeed, until sacrificed for road improvements, the trees screened The Broadway from The Steyne.

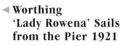

◄ **Worthing**
'Lady Rowena' Sails
from the Pier 1921

71464

Steamer trips from the
pier were highlights of
many seaside holidays all
over England. The 'Lady
Rowena' was a well
known paddle steamer.

▼ **West Tarring**
High Street 1890 22722
Owned and restored by
the Sussex Archeological
Society, Parsonage Row,
a 15th-century Wealden
house, is part of a village
that retained its identity,
despite being swamped
by Worthing's northward
expansion during the
1920s.

◄ **West Tarring**
St Andrew's Church
1890 22721
This mainly 13th century
church, with its broad
tower and slim spire,
has fine stalls and
misericords, as well as
some modern mosaic
work.

Inland Sussex:

The County Towns and the Market Towns

Chichester
The Market Cross 1890 22618
With a plan based on its Roman predecessor,
Noviomagus, this fine walled city is divided into
quarters by North, South, East and West Streets,
which all meet at the splendid Market Cross in the
centre of the town. The south-west section is
dominated by the Norman cathedral, established
here after 1072, when the Bishopric was moved
here from Selsey. Bishop Storey built this superb
Cross in 1501, on market land bought from the
mayor and burgesses for £10, specifically so that
'the poore peple shall here after stand or sell eny
Chafer (goods) Within the said Crosse' free of
market tolls.

Chichester, East Street 1890 22622
The Greek Doric columns and pediment of the old Corn Exchange of 1832, now a McDonalds restaurant, are astonishingly out of scale in this quiet street of smaller-scale Georgian fronts.

Chichester, Canon Gate, South Street 1890 22623
The south-west section of Chichester is dominated by the Norman cathedral, established here after 1072, when the Bishopric was moved here from Selsey. The twin-archwayed late 15th-century gatehouse is Canon Gate, which leads into the Cathedral precincts. The houses in South Street become smaller in scale than in the other three streets meeting at the central Market Cross.

Lewes, High Street 1898 41906

Lewes, the medieval guardian of the gap through the South Downs cut by the River Ouse, occupies a fine hilltop site which produces a superb townscape. Its Cluniac priory was one of the richest in medieval England, and its founder William de Warenne's castle dominates the town and distant views. Until the mid 19th century this vista was closed by a town hall in the middle of the road. Apart from this loss, little has changed.

Lewes, School Hill 1903 50924

At the Market Street junction, the High Street starts dropping steeply to School Hill. The ornate lamp standard was replaced a few years later by an equally elaborate War Memorial. In the distance is the tower of Harvey's Brewery.

**Lewes
Cliffe High Street
Looking West 1894**
34504
St Thomas Becket
church is at the east
end of Cliffe High
Street, which runs west
to cross the Ouse into
School Hill and Lewes
proper. Cliffe is noted
for Harvey's Bridge
Quay Brewery, a mostly
Victorian building.

Lewes, School Hill 1921 70214

On School Hill, several houses on the left, including the bow window, are clad in mathematical tiles, hanging tiles that simulate brick. They are difficult to tell from real brickwork if well done.

Arundel, The Castle from the River 1902 48790

The castle, much enlarged by the Dukes of Norfolk, along with their Roman Catholic cathedral, dominates this picturesque hill town, giving it a distinctly French character in distant views. The bridge over the River Arun was replaced by the present stone parapeted one in 1935. On the right are the ruins of the Maison Dieu of about 1400, possibly a small monastic house dissolved by Henry VIII in 1546.

▲ Arundel The Castle and Town from the Air c1955
A62001

Like Lewes, Arundel was established by a Norman baron, this time Roger de Montgomery, to guard a river gap in the South Downs, in this case the Arun. Halfway along the castle, Henry II's shell keep on the Norman Motte or mound divides the two baileys, the right-hand one filled with the massive Victorian rebuild. The aerial view brings out the medieval town plan well.

◀ **Arundel**
The High Street, Looking South 1908 60153
This view looks downhill towards the former market place. The castle wall on the left was mostly rebuilt in the 19th century. Architecturally, little has changed: the view is now merely cluttered by motor vehicles, parked or moving.

**Arundel
The High Street 1902**
48792
At the bottom end of
the High Street, in the
old market place, pride
of place goes to the
water pump crowned
by a gas street light.
The gabled building was
newly built at this time.

◀ **Arundel**
The High Street and the War Memorial 1923 73629
In 1923 the town commemorated its dead of the Great War by building this fine war memorial. The water pump has gone, and the Norfolk Arms hotel apparently has a side line in motor car repairs.

◄ **Battle**
The High Street looking towards the Abbey 1921 71507
The long High Street curves gently towards the triangular market place in front of the Abbey gatehouse. The Ford Service Depot on the right, with the two Fords parked nearby, is still a car showroom.

▼ **Battle**
The Abbey Gatehouse, 1927
80411
William the Conqueror, having beaten and killed the Anglo-Danish King Harold on Senlac Hill in 1066, vowed to found an abbey on the site of the great battle, known as the Battle of Hastings. William the Conqueror gave the Abbey a market which was held in front of the Abbey's gates, although the present magnificent Gatehouse was built for Abbot Alan of Ketling in 1338 to replace the Norman one.

◄ **Battle**
The Abbey, The Abbot's Great Hall 1910 62981
Now part of a girls' school, the Abbot's Great Hall is its centrepiece, originally of the 15th century. It has now been made more medieval than it was: the minstrels' gallery and the massive fireplace were added in the 1850s by Henry Clutton.

Battle, The High Street from the Abbey Gatehouse 1910 62991
The old market place is more of a grassy village green at this time. The High Street is relatively unchanged. Astonishingly, the plot boundaries, if not the buildings themselves, were established in the late 11th century.

Billingshurst, High Street 1909 62165
This small town grew up on the course of the Roman road from London to Chichester, later known as Stane (or stone paved) Street. In later years it developed as a small coaching town on the London road. Despite the traffic, the buildings mostly remain; even Field's is still a hardware shop. The buildings beyond The King's Head have gone, and the wall on the right has been replaced by a row of lock-up shops.

Billingshurst, Mill Lane 1907 58206
Its Anglo-Saxon name means 'wooded hill in the territory of Billa's people'. This rural lane is now unrecognisable, being a tarmac road leading to a car park, the library and a council estate, although the church with its broach spire and the High Street houses on the skyline remain.

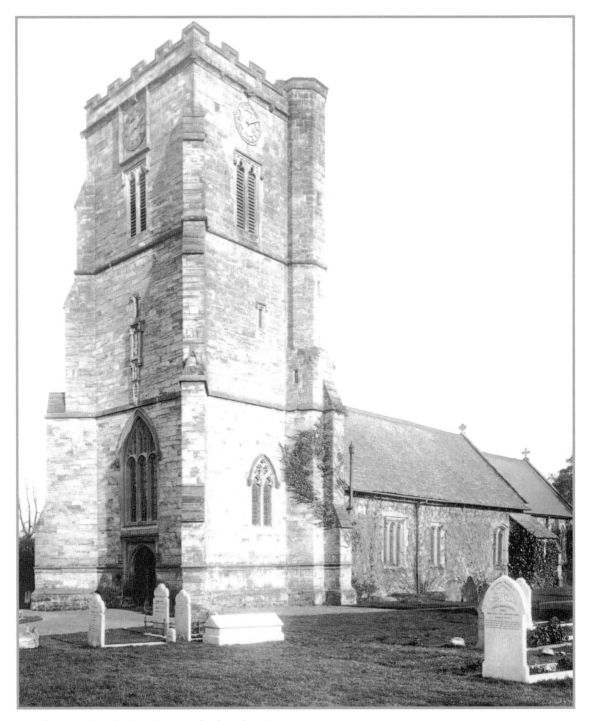

Crawley, St John the Baptist Parish Church 1903 50765
This old coaching town on the London to Brighton road had the misfortune to be designated a New Town in 1947.
Now swamped by housing estates, the High Street was mainly pedestrianised. However, a substantial amount was
demolished, and more is soon to go at the south end. Set back behind the High Street, the church looks
reassuringly medieval amid the modernity of Crawley, but in fact only the nave wall is: the tower was rebuilt in
1807 and the rest in 1880.

Crawley, The High Street and the George Hotel 1905 53313
Elements of this small historic coaching town still remain, including the well-restored George Hotel and its inn sign on gallows spanning the now mainly pedestrianised road. However, much else in this view has gone.

Crawley, The High Street 1903 50757
The left-hand building was an encroachment into the medieval market place, a process whereby market stalls were gradually replaced by permanent buildings. Here, the New Town swept them away, but they survive in Arundel and East Grinstead.

Crawley
The Fair 1905 53326
Although a market is still held in the High Street, there are no cattle fairs any more. This picture evokes a different world and a very different Crawley from today's seething New Town of more than 60,000 people.

◄ **Crawley**
The High Street,
North-East Side 1905
53314
Even further north along the east side, much has now gone, with the New Town's modern shopping centre reaching the old High Street proper; but some of the spaciousness in the distance remains.

Crawley
The High Street 1903
50759

A little further along the Burgess House Furnisher building, a 15th-century open hall and cross-wing house, is now well restored. Its genuine timber-framing with close set timbers has been exposed and the sham gable timbers removed.

Crawley
Brighton Road looking across the Railway Crossing 1903 50762

In the middle distance the London Brighton and South Coast Railway lines cut across Brighton Road on a level crossing. Between the 1901 bank on the left and the foreground is now the Imperial Cinema of 1928.

Crawley
The Albany Temperance Hotel
1907 57793

The Victorian temperance movement was sufficiently concerned at the drunkenness of commercial travellers to set up and encourage the building of alcohol-free hotels everywhere for them. One wonders what degree of success they had.

**East Grinstead
High Street, South
Side 1923** 73352
This is reputed by East
Grinsteaders to be one
of the longest
continuous rows of
medieval timber-framed
buildings in the country.
It is certainly a very fine
range, and one, the
bookshop, has its
framing decorated with
bark panels.

East Grinstead, High Street Looking East 1904 52900

The town, now mercifully by-passed, has a remarkably complete High Street, considering the volume of traffic that used to choke it en route to the coast. This view looking east is virtually unchanged. The trees and low wall in the distance belong to the grounds of Sackville College, a wonderful quadrangle in mellow local sandstone, founded in 1617 as almshouses.

East Grinstead, High Street 1904 52901

There is a splendid proportion of medieval and Tudor timber-framed houses; it is even more astonishing that the market infill between Middle Row and the High Street survived traffic imperatives. This view looks west to the town centre. The white gable represents market encroachment; it survived the 20th century's obsession with clearing the path for motor vehicles. The superb jettied and close-studded timber framed house is Cromwell House.

East Grinstead, High Street, West End 1910 62800
As we look east from near London Road, we can see the layout of the wide 13th-century market place. Market encroachment blocks the view, with a new lane formed between it and the original plots fronting Middle Row on the right.

East Grinstead, London Road from the High Street Junction 1891 29587
If the High Street represents remarkable survival, London Road does not. The fine Italianate stucco building of about 1850 on the right survives, and is now Lloyds Bank. Virtually everything else has gone.

◄ **East Grinstead London Road, looking South 1904** 52902
This view was taken further down the hill and looking south. The buildings on the right survive, while the two on the left were rebuilt in the 1930s as Whitehall, a grandiose Art Deco range in white Portland stone.

◄ **East Grinstead London Road looking North-West 1914** 66750
By 1914 the Cinema De Luxe had appeared at the south end of London Road. Some of the buildings on the left further downhill remain, but the street was largely rebuilt in the 1930s suburban shopping parade style.

▼ **East Grinstead London Road, looking South 1914** 66751
By 1914 the Cinema De Luxe had a rival 200 yards away, the Whitehall, which prominently advertises its wares to the fascination of passers-by. Further up is a motor garage, so the modern age has indeed arrived.

◄ **East Grinstead Hermitage Lane, Looking North towards the Church 1904** 52907
Hermitage Lane cuts steeply down through the sandstone. This evocative view, wholly unchanged today, is barely 200 yards from the busy High Street. The soaring parish church tower, carefully rebuilt following its collapse in 1785, closes the view.

▼ **Hailsham, High Street, 1902** 48483
Hailsham was a small market town before the railway arrived, after which there was considerable expansion. Much of its wealth and subsequent Victorian building was a result of prosperity based on rope, sacking and string making. The 20th century has added modern shopping centres and a leisure complex. This view of Hailsham captures The String Town in its Victorian prosperity.

▼ **Horsham, The Causeway 1898** 41923
Yet another town that has benefited from a by-pass, and is now rediscovering itself without constant through traffic. The Causeway always was a tranquil haven amid the chaos, but imaginative pedestrianisation and traffic calming schemes have made Horsham a delight again, particularly around Carfax. The view is remarkably similar now, a century later, as the limes had to be replanted in 1940. Cut off from the bustling town centre by the old town hall, this lane feels more like a village street.

▲ **Horsham West Street, looking East 1936** 87228
West Street is now pedestrianised, but the Chart and Lawrence department store and Lloyds Bank on the opposite corner are still trading. To the right, out of view, is Carfax, a splendid irregular market place.

◄ **Midhurst
The South End 1912**
64908
This view looks up South Street past the old mill pond, towards the tangled medieval core of the town around its much restored church; the celebrated Spread Eagle Hotel is behind the trees on the left.

**Midhurst
The King Edward
Sanatorium 1907**
58334
Set in woods two miles
north of Midhurst, the
King Edward Sanatorium
(1903-6, by Charles
Holden) is vast but built
in a humane Tudorish
style. Most rooms have
the benefit of the views
to the South Downs.

Midhurst, North Street 1921 70084
Midhurst is a town of contrasts, with an early medieval core around the church, west of the Norman castle earthworks on St Anne's Hill, and the wide North Street, a later medieval planned market place. This wide, straight road leads to the intricacies of the rest of Midhurst. The late-Victorian towered building has been replaced by a nasty 1960s supermarket building, but otherwise little has changed.

Petworth, Saddlers Row 1906 54365
A small medieval market town, Petworth is a delightful tangle of lanes and alleys. Saddlers Row remains intact, apart from the tall chimney, but the saddler has gone - it is now an antique shop - and Pellett's is now a restaurant. Times change, and the lane to the left leads to Petworth's main car park.

Petworth, Lombard Street 1900 44979
The high walls of Petworth House dominate the west side of the town. Unusually, Petworth House itself is just
beyond these walls instead of in the middle of its park, and this gives the town almost a French air. The cobbles of
this street remain, but the shops have become houses. The church spire was demolished in 1947. Not medieval, it
was installed in 1827, apparently using a design for another church.

Inland Sussex:
Villages, Castles and New Towns

Bodiam
Bodiam Castle 1890 25390
Bodiam is dominated by one of the most picturesque castles in England, set within a broad moat filled with golden carp. The castle, at the medieval limit of navigation for the River Rother, was presumably licensed in 1385 following French raids on Rye and Winchelsea. It became a picturesque ruin after a brief 1643 Civil War siege, until Lord Curzon bought the castle in 1919, restored it impeccably and passed it to the National Trust.

◀ **Bodiam**
Oast Houses c1965
B128018
Oast houses are common in the Weald of Sussex as well as in Kent, and indeed wherever hops are grown. The buildings are usually circular; heated air passed through the hops laid on the drying floor and out through the cowl hood.

◄ Amberley
Vinsons Tea Lawns and Caravan Park c1965 A44066

Amberley, with its medieval castle/palace of the Bishops of Chichester has been a popular tourist spot for years, and now has the Amberley Museum in the former chalk pits, a fascinating industrial heritage collection. This most evocative photograph calls to mind the simpler pleasures of a day out in the 1960s: the quaint, dated name 'Tea Lawn', the women sitting drinking tea, the men and boys restless and on the move.

▼ Bramber
The Village looking West c1890 22724

Once as important as Arundel or Lewes, Bramber is now merely a village, the market centre having migrated to nearby Steyning. Now by-passed, Bramber has recovered some of its tranquillity, but it has lost the rough-hewn workaday look we see in this view. In the distance is the tree-clad hill of Bramber Castle with the stone tooth of its keep.

◄ Bramber
The Village c1955
B179014

The Tea Gardens have long closed, but peeping over the roof is the squat battlemented tower of de Braose's Norman church, brutally treated subsequently, but notable for the 1070s tower arch capitals: wonderfully crude carving.

Bramber, The Castle Ruins c1955 B179009
Bramber was once the main town of one of the Sussex Rapes, or Anglo-Saxon administrative areas, and the seat of William de Braose's Norman castle guarding the Adur gap through the Downs. By 1100 he had added a stone keep to his castle, which was built on a natural hill overlooking the Adur. Only a 75 ft high fragment and some stretches of bailey wall remain on this refreshingly unmanicured site.

Burgess Hill, Church Road c1950 B284007
From its beginnings as a railway station amid fields, the town has grown and continues to grow dramatically. Church Road's late 19th-century shopping parade leads from the station to the steepled 1860s church, built to minister a burgeoning commuter town.

Crowborough, The Cross 1900 44928
In the 1870s a Dr Prince persuaded Lord Abergavenny, the landowner, to develop this area, bordering the Ashdown Forest and set at a healthy 800 ft above sea level, as a health resort. It is now a commuter town, but retains many of the spacious villas of its health resort days. The 1880s Tudor-style buildings on the left give some impression of the high quality of much of Crowborough's development. The bank is now the Nat West, and beyond the right-hand buildings is the modern Fernbank Shopping Centre.

**Goodwood
The Race Course
1904** 52291
'Glorious Goodwood',
one of the great
advertising slogans,
usually lives up to its
name, and the racing
that takes place here,
high on the South
Downs and a mile north
of Goodwood House,
is usually blessed with
wonderful weather.
Racing here started in
1802, and the horse-
shoe-shaped course
was graced by this
jaunty two-deck
grandstand in 1904.

▼ **Haywards Heath, South Road 1954** H252012
Haywards Heath grew up as a commuter town on the London, Brighton and
South Coast Railway, whose isolated 1841 station for Cuckfield formed its
nucleus. The Heath itself is much reduced, but in places you can still find the
early spacious villas where they have not been swept away for blocks of flats.
Facing Victoria Park, these 1930s shops and flats combine attempts at rendered
Moderne architecture with safer Neo-Georgian sash windows and brick.

▼ **High Salvington, The Old Windmill 1919** 68994
Worthing, like a tide of building, washed east, west and north before and after
the Second World War. High Salvington, a hamlet on the downs, is now
swallowed up, as is the Findon Valley below to the east; in effect it is a suburb cut off by the teeming A27. Built in the early 18th century, this post mill
stopped grinding corn in 1897, and deteriorated badly after this photograph
was taken. It was rescued and meticulously restored between 1987 and 1997,
and can now mill again.

▲ **High Salvington
The Downs 1919** 68995
In 1919 Worthing had not
yet sprawled up the valley
below Salvington Hill, and
you could look across to
Cissbury Ring without the
neat, but characterless,
housing of Findon Valley
in between.

◀ **Ifield**
Looking towards the Church 1905 53330
Crawley's expansion as a planned New Town after 1947 took in hamlets right up to Ifield. It was a small and sleepy Sussex village, until then remote in the rolling landscape of the western Weald, a landscape of small dense hedged fields and oak trees. Behind the photographer is now the Ifield neighbourhood of Crawley New Town, but looking towards the church of this tiny hamlet the view is virtually unchanged.

◄ **Lancing College from beyond the Old Road Bridge 1890** 22733
The towering chapel of this school dominates the landscape for miles around; its position is wonderful, high above where the South Downs are cut deep by the Adur valley on its way to the sea. The chapel was only completed twenty years after this view was taken. This wooden bridge survives. Authorised by an Act of Parliament in 1781, it carried traffic until 1971.

◀ **Lancing College 1890** 22734
Founded by Nathanial Woodard, then curate at nearby New Shoreham, Lancing was one of fifteen schools he established, including Ardingly and Hurstpierpoint in Sussex. R C Carpenter's school buildings, begun in 1854, were occupied in 1858 and added to subsequently. When his father died in 1855, R H Carpenter designed the soaring chapel, which was started in 1868 and is seen here half-finished.

▼ **Parham House**
The South Front 1894 34403
The northern lee along the foot of the South Downs escarpment always seems to have been a favoured location for country houses. Examples from west to east include Burton Park, Parham itself, Wiston Park, Firle Place and Folkington Manor. Some, including Parham, can be seen from the South Downs Way. The foundation stone of this Elizabethan E-plan sandstone mansion was laid in 1577 by Thomas Palmer, the two-year-old grandson of the owner, Sir Thomas Palmer.

◀ **Parham House**
The Portrait Gallery 1896 38196
Parham was restored and re-Elizabethanised this century. Its Long Gallery, used for winter promenades among the ancestral portraits, is 160 ft long, and the 19th-century ceiling was replaced by a more accurately-proportioned one.

Pulborough, Swan's Corner 1921 70065
The town-village grew up where the Roman Stane Street crossed the River Arun. The church and a cluster of old houses are at the top of the hill, and more old buildings are on the river bank, east and west of the Bognor Road river bridge. Despite being at the junction through which traffic to Bognor pours, this timber-framed cottage survives. The Swan Hotel was replaced in 1961 by an ill-judged stone and boarded giant bungalow of a pub.

Pulborough, Clement's Bridge 1906 56746
The Rother and Arun bridges are a remarkable survival and justly renowned: mostly medieval, some have until recently had to survive increasingly heavy traffic. Both Pulborough's and Stopham's medieval bridges are now fortunately by-passed and left as footbridges.

Rottingdean, The Village Pond c1955 R62003
Rottingdean, the valley of Rota's people, is cut off from its vast neighbour, Brighton, by steep chalk downs and sea cliffs. Although within Brighton's boundaries since 1928, it retains much of its character, despite Saltdean's sprawl colliding from the east. With Kipling's 'blunt, bow-headed, whale-backed Downs' surrounding it, the village runs up a valley from the sea, climaxing beyond the High Street on the Green with its pond, where Kipling lived.

Shoreham, The Norfolk Suspension Bridge 1919 69000
The River Adur ports had a chequered history. Anglo-Saxon Bramber was superseded by early Norman Old Shoreham, nearer the river mouth, and then by New Shoreham, which was itself half washed away by 1400. Kingston Buci had probably already taken over further along the shingle spit. What a tragic loss this superb 1833 suspension bridge was. Designed by William Tierney Clarke, it was replaced in 1923.

Upper Beeding, The Convent of the Blessed Sacrament c1955 U40026

Upper Beeding is in effect a suburb of Bramber. It is mostly nondescript, apart from its parish church at the north end, overlooking the river. Until Henry VIII's Dissolution of the monasteries, this was the monks' church of Sele Priory, founded here by William de Braose in 1075. The Tower School is a quirky building, perhaps a counterpoint to Bramber Castle on the other side of the Adur. Dating from about 1880, it has corner towers with conical roofs and full machicolated battlements.

Burwash, A Group of Friends c1890 B291001

A linear village along a ridge between the Rother and Dudwell rivers, Burwash prospered in the Wealden iron industry. Then it declined, and found an unsavoury niche as a smuggling and sheep-rustling centre. Here are a group of young citizens of Burwash with rural baby carts (hardly prams) photographed over a century ago. This view freezes yesterday's rural community during the era before the commuter changed everything for ever.

Index

The Francis Frith Collection publishes over 100 new titles each year. A selection of those currently available is listed below. For latest catalogue please contact The Francis Frith Collection.
Town Books 96 pages, approximately 75 photos. **County and Themed Books** 128 pages, approximately 135 photos (unless specified). Pocket Albums are miniature editions of Frith local history books 128 pages, approximately 95 photos.

Accrington Old and New
Alderley Edge and Wilmslow
Amersham, Chesham and Rickmansworth
Andover
Around Abergavenny
Around Alton
Aylesbury
Barnstaple
Bedford
Bedfordshire
Berkshire Living Memories
Berkshire Pocket Album
Blackpool Pocket Album
Bognor Regis
Bournemouth
Bradford
Bridgend
Bridport
Brighton and Hove
Bristol
Buckinghamshire
Calne Living Memories
Camberley Pocket Album
Canterbury Cathedral
Cardiff Old and New
Chatham and the Medway Towns
Chelmsford
Chepstow Then and Now
Cheshire
Cheshire Living Memories
Chester
Chesterfield
Chigwell
Christchurch
Churches of East Cornwall
Clevedon
Clitheroe
Corby Living Memories
Cornish Coast
Cornwall Living Memories
Cotswold Living Memories
Cotswold Pocket Album
Coulsdon, Chipstead and Woodmanstern
County Durham
Cromer, Sheringham and Holt
Dartmoor Pocket Album
Derby
Derbyshire
Derbyshire Living Memories
Devon
Devon Churches
Dorchester

Dorset Coast Pocket Album
Dorset Living Memories
Dorset Villages
Down the Dart
Down the Severn
Down the Thames
Dunmow, Thaxted and Finchingfield
Durham
East Anglia Pocket Album
East Devon
East Grinstead
Edinburgh
Ely and The Fens
Essex Pocket Album
Essex Second Selection
Essex: The London Boroughs
Exeter
Exmoor
Falmouth
Farnborough, Fleet and Aldershot
Folkestone
Frome
Furness and Cartmel Peninsulas
Glamorgan
Glasgow
Glastonbury
Gloucester
Gloucestershire
Greater Manchester
Guildford
Hailsham
Hampshire
Harrogate
Hastings and Bexhill
Haywards Heath Living Memories
Heads of the Valleys
Heart of Lancashire Pocket Album
Helston
Herefordshire
Horsham
Humberside Pocket Album
Huntingdon, St Neots and St Ives
Hythe, Romney Marsh and Ashford
Ilfracombe
Ipswich Pocket Album
Isle of Wight
Isle of Wight Living Memories
King's Lynn
Kingston upon Thames
Lake District Pocket Album
Lancashire Living Memories
Lancashire Villages

Available from your local bookshop or from the publisher

The Francis Frith Collection Titles (continued)

Lancaster, Morecambe and Heysham Pocket Album
Leeds Pocket Album
Leicester
Leicestershire
Lincolnshire Living Memoires
Lincolnshire Pocket Album
Liverpool and Merseyside
London Pocket Album
Ludlow
Maidenhead
Maidstone
Malmesbury
Manchester Pocket Album
Marlborough
Matlock
Merseyside Living Memories
Nantwich and Crewe
New Forest
Newbury Living Memories
Newquay to St Ives
North Devon Living Memories
North London
North Wales
North Yorkshire
Northamptonshire
Northumberland
Northwich
Nottingham
Nottinghamshire Pocket Album
Oakham
Odiham Then and Now
Oxford Pocket Album
Oxfordshire
Padstow
Pembrokeshire
Penzance
Petersfield Then and Now
Plymouth
Poole and Sandbanks
Preston Pocket Album
Ramsgate Old and New
Reading Pocket Album
Redditch Living Memories
Redhill to Reigate
Richmond
Ringwood
Rochdale
Romford Pocket Album
Salisbury Pocket Album
Scotland
Scottish Castles
Sevenoaks and Tonbridge
Sheffield and South Yorkshire Pocket Album
Shropshire
Somerset
South Devon Coast
South Devon Living Memories
South East London

Southampton Pocket Album
Southend Pocket Album
Southport
Southwold to Aldeburgh
Stourbridge Living Memories
Stratford upon Avon
Stroud
Suffolk
Suffolk Pocket Album
Surrey Living Memories
Sussex
Sutton
Swanage and Purbeck
Swansea Pocket Album
Swindon Living Memories
Taunton
Teignmouth
Tenby and Saundersfoot
Tiverton
Torbay
Truro
Uppingham
Villages of Kent
Villages of Surrey
Villages of Sussex Pocket Album
Wakefield and the Five Towns Living Memories
Warrington
Warwick
Warwickshire Pocket Album
Wellingborough Living Memories
Wells
Welsh Castles
West Midlands Pocket Album
West Wiltshire Towns
West Yorkshire
Weston-super-Mare
Weymouth
Widnes and Runcorn
Wiltshire Churches
Wiltshire Living Memories
Wiltshire Pocket Album
Wimborne
Winchester Pocket Album
Windermere
Windsor
Wirral
Wokingham and Bracknell
Woodbridge
Worcester
Worcestershire
Worcestershire Living Memories
Wyre Forest
York Pocket Album
Yorkshire
Yorkshire Coastal Memories
Yorkshire Dales
Yorkshire Revisited

See Frith books on the internet at www.francisfrith.com

FRITH PRODUCTS & SERVICES

Francis Frith would doubtless be pleased to know that the pioneering publishing venture he started in 1860 still continues today. Over a hundred and forty years later, The Francis Frith Collection continues in the same innovative tradition and is now one of the foremost publishers of vintage photographs in the world. Some of the current activities include:

INTERIOR DECORATION

Today Frith's photographs can be seen framed and as giant wall murals in thousands of pubs, restaurants, hotels, banks, retail stores and other public buildings throughout the country. In every case they enhance the unique local atmosphere of the places they depict and provide reminders of gentler days in an increasingly busy and frenetic world.

PRODUCT PROMOTIONS

Frith products are used by many major companies to promote the sales of their own products or to reinforce their own history and heritage. Frith promotions have been used by Hovis bread, Courage beers, Scots Porage Oats, Colman's mustard, Cadbury's foods, Mellow Birds coffee, Dunhill pipe tobacco, Guinness, and Bulmer's Cider.

GENEALOGY AND FAMILY HISTORY

As the interest in family history and roots grows world-wide, more and more people are turning to Frith's photographs of Great Britain for images of the towns, villages and streets where their ancestors lived; and, of course, photographs of the churches and chapels where their ancestors were christened, married and buried are an essential part of every genealogy tree and family album.

FRITH PRODUCTS

All Frith photographs are available Framed or just as Mounted Prints and Posters (size 23 x 16 inches). These may be ordered from the address below. Other products available are- Address Books, Calendars, Jigsaws, Canvas Prints, Notelets and local and prestige books.

THE INTERNET

Already ninety thousand Frith photographs can be viewed and purchased on the internet through the Frith websites and a myriad of partner sites.

For more detailed information on Frith companies and products, look at this site:
www.francisfrith.com

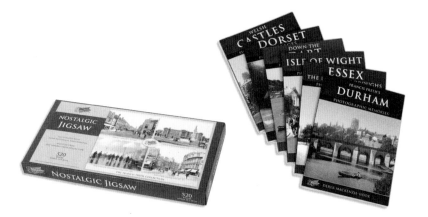

See the complete list of Frith Books at: www.francisfrith.com
This web site is regularly updated with the latest list of publications from The Francis Frith Collection. If you wish to buy books relating to another part of the country that your local bookshop does not stock, you may purchase on-line.

For further information, trade, or author enquiries please contact us at the address below:
The Francis Frith Collection, Unit 6, Oakley Business Park, Wylye Road, Dinton, Wiltshire SP3 5EU.
Tel: +44 (0)1722 716 376 Fax: +44 (0)1722 716 881 Email: sales@francisfrith.co.uk

---

See Frith products on the internet at www.francisfrith.com

FREE PRINT OF YOUR CHOICE

Mounted Print
Overall size 14 x 11 inches (355 x 280mm)

Choose any Frith photograph in this book.
Simply complete the Voucher opposite and return it with your remittance for £3.50 (to cover postage and handling) and we will print the photograph of your choice in SEPIA (size 11 x 8 inches) and supply it in a cream mount with a burgundy rule line (overall size 14 x 11 inches).
Please note: aerial photographs and photographs with a reference number starting with a "Z" are not Frith photographs and cannot be supplied under this offer. Offer valid for delivery to one UK address only.

PLUS: **Order additional Mounted Prints at HALF PRICE - £9.50 each** (normally £19.00)
If you would like to order more Frith prints from this book, possibly as gifts for friends and family, you can buy them at half price (with no additional postage and handling costs).

PLUS: **Have your Mounted Prints framed**
For an extra £18.00 per print you can have your mounted print(s) framed in an elegant polished wood and gilt moulding, overall size 16 x 13 inches (no additional postage and handling required).

IMPORTANT!

These special prices are only available if you use this form to order. You must use the ORIGINAL VOUCHER on this page (no copies permitted). We can only despatch to one UK address. This offer cannot be combined with any other offer.

Send completed Voucher form to:
The Francis Frith Collection, Unit 6, Oakley Business Park, Wylye Road, Dinton, Wiltshire SP3 5EU

CHOOSE A PHOTOGRAPH FROM THIS BOOK

Voucher for **FREE** *and Reduced Price Frith Prints*

Please do not photocopy this voucher. Only the original is valid, so please fill it in, cut it out and return it to us with your order.

Picture ref no	Page no	Qty	Mounted @ £9.50	Framed + £18.00	Total Cost £
		1	Free of charge*	£	£
			£9.50	£	£
			£9.50	£	£
			£9.50	£	£
			£9.50	£	£
			£9.50	£	£

Please allow 28 days for delivery. Offer available to one UK address only

* Post & handling		£3.50
Total Order Cost		£

Title of this book . . . .

I enclose a cheque/postal order for £ . . . .
made payable to 'The Francis Frith Collection'

OR please debit my Mastercard / Visa / Maestro card, details below

Card Number:

Issue No (Maestro only):   Valid from (Maestro):

Card Security Number: Expires:

Signature:

Name Mr/Mrs/Ms . . . .

Address . . . .

. . . .

. . . .

. . . . Postcode . . . .

Daytime Tel No . . . .

Email . . . .

1-85937-184-1   Valid to 31/12/14

Can you help us with information about any of the Frith photographs in this book?

We are gradually compiling an historical record for each of the photographs in the Frith archive. It is always fascinating to find out the names of the people shown in the pictures, as well as insights into the shops, buildings and other features depicted.

If you recognize anyone in the photographs in this book, or if you have information not already included in the author's caption, do let us know. We would love to hear from you, and will try to publish it in future books or articles.

An Invitation from The Francis Frith Collection to Share Your Memories

The 'Share Your Memories' feature of our website allows members of the public to add personal memories relating to the places featured in our photographs, or comment on others already added. Seeing a place from your past can rekindle forgotten or long held memories. Why not visit the website, find photographs of places you know well and add YOUR story for others to read and enjoy? We would love to hear from you!

www.francisfrith.com/memories

Our production team

Frith books are produced by a small dedicated team at offices near Salisbury. Most have worked with the Frith Collection for many years. All have in common one quality: they have a passion for the Frith Collection.

Frith Books and Gifts

We have a wide range of books and gifts available on our website utilising our photographic archive, many of which can be individually personalised.

www.francisfrith.com